Mapping the Milky Way

Nicole Sipe

Contributing Author

Allison Duarte, M.A.

Consultants

Tamieka Grizzle, Ed.D.
K–5 STEM Lab Instructor
Harmony Leland Elementary School

Mark Reid
Astronomer
Smithsonian

Publishing Credits

Rachelle Cracchiolo, M.S.Ed., *Publisher*
Conni Medina, M.A.Ed., *Managing Editor*
Diana Kenney, M.A.Ed., NBCT, *Content Director*
Véronique Bos, *Creative Director*
June Kikuchi, *Content Director*
Robin Erickson, *Art Director*
Seth Rogers, *Editor*
Mindy Duits, *Senior Graphic Designer*
Smithsonian Science Education Center

Image Credits: p.9 Pasieka/Science Source; p.11 Granger Academic; p.12 Science History Images/Alamy; p.13 Shootmybusiness/Shutterstock; p.14 NASA; p.15 Emilio Segrè Visual Archives/American Institute of Physics/Science Source; p.17 (top) Gianni Tortoli/Getty Images; p.17 (bottom) Stock Montage/Getty Images; p.19, p.21, 24 (bottom) NASA; p.23 (all), 25 (bottom) Science Source; pp.24–25 NASA/JPL-Caltech; p.26 Detlev van Ravensnaay/Science Source; p.27 Mark Williamson/Science Source; all other images from iStock and/or Shutterstock.

Library of Congress Cataloging-in-Publication Data

Names: Sipe, Nicole, author.
Title: Mapping the Milky Way / Nicole Sipe.
Description: Huntington Beach, CA : Teacher Created Materials, [2018] | Audience: K to grade 3. | Includes index.
Identifiers: LCCN 2017056322 (print) | LCCN 2017059542 (ebook) | ISBN 9781493869299 (e-book) | ISBN 9781493866892 (pbk.)
Subjects: LCSH: Milky Way--Juvenile literature. | Galaxies--Measurement--Juvenile literature. | Stars--Juvenile literature. | Astronomy--Charts, diagrams, etc.--Juvenile literature.
Classification: LCC QB857.7 (ebook) | LCC QB857.7 .S57 2018 (print) | DDC 523.1/13--dc23
LC record available at https://lccn.loc.gov/2017056322

Smithsonian

Teacher Created Materials

5301 Oceanus Drive
Huntington Beach, CA 92649-1030
www.tcmpub.com

ISBN 978-1-4938-6689-2
© 2019 Teacher Created Materials, Inc.

Table of Contents

Mapping the Impossible

Imagine you are standing in the middle of a large forest. Can you count all the trees in the forest from where you stand? You can count the trees that you can see. You can even guess how many trees are in the forest. But the forest is large, and you are standing in the middle of it. So counting all the trees seems like an impossible task!

This is what it is like for scientists who are trying to create a map of the Milky Way. It is a very difficult thing to map! The Milky Way is huge. Also, Earth is part of it. And then there is the pesky problem of the gas and dust at the center of the Milky Way that block our view. How do we make a map of the Milky Way under these difficult conditions? A lot of people have worked to figure this out.

Home Sweet Home

The next time you are outdoors on a clear night, look up. You might see a large, faint band of light streaking the dark sky. That is part of the Milky Way!

The Milky Way is our home. It is the name of our **galaxy**. A galaxy is a group of stars. The Milky Way has billions of stars! It also has clouds, gas, and even dust.

Our **solar system** is part of the Milky Way. Earth, the seven other planets, our moon, and the sun are all part of this galaxy.

For many years, people thought that Earth was the center of the galaxy. We now know that this is not true. The sun is about two-thirds of the way from the center of the Milky Way. Our solar system makes a complete trip around the Milky Way every 215 million years. The last time Earth was in the same part of the Milky Way as it is now, dinosaurs roamed the planet.

a band of the Milky Way as seen from Earth

Twinkle, Twinkle, Little Star

Look up at the stars at night. Do they look like they are twinkling? This happens because you are looking at the stars through a thin layer of gases that surround Earth. This layer is called the **atmosphere**. It bends the light in random directions, making the stars look like twinkling lights.

The Milky Way is a spiral galaxy. From above, it would look like a spiral with a bulge in the center. It has four bright arms that wrap around to form a disk shape. Think of a giant space pinwheel. Unlike a pinwheel, the Milky Way is never still. It is always moving and changing. Earth and the rest of our solar system are near one of the arms of the Milky Way.

The center of the Milky Way is much harder to see than the arms. Thick layers of dust and gas block our view. Some scientists think that a big black hole is in the center. A black hole is an area in space with gravity so strong that light cannot escape.

The halo is the outer edge of the Milky Way. Old stars and dark matter are found in this hot and gassy area. Dark matter is invisible. But we know it is there because its gravity pulls on the matter we can see.

A black hole is so strong that it can pull in anything that gets close to it. It can even merge with other black holes!

A spiral galaxy looks kind of like a pinwheel.

How Big?

We know that the Milky Way is huge. It is so big that most people cannot even imagine its size. Our sun is just one of about 100 billion stars in the Milky Way. To understand how many stars that is, we need to start by comparing it to something smaller.

Think of a grain of sand. Imagine how small it is. You can fit thousands of grains of sand in your hand. It would take 100 dump trucks to hold 100 billion grains of sand. Now, instead of tiny grains of sand, imagine stars the size of our sun. That's a lot of stars!

All these stars are not close together. In fact, they are very far apart. Stars may look small in the sky, but that is only because they are very far away from Earth. The sun looks like the biggest star in the sky because it is so close. There are a lot of stars in the galaxy that would make the sun seem tiny if they were closer to Earth.

Hipparchus looks at the stars.

MATHEMATICS

The Man and the Moon

Ancient Greek **astronomer** Hipparchus (hih-PAHR-kiss) wanted to find out how far the moon was from Earth. To do this, he used data from a solar eclipse. A solar eclipse is when the sun, moon, and Earth all line up. The moon blocks the sun's light. In different places on Earth, the moon covers different amounts of the sun. Hipparchus used this to calculate the distance between the moon and Earth.

Points of View

The Milky Way is hard to map because of its size. Over the years, scientists have tried different ways to **chart** the stars. It is thrilling each time they learn something new. It is like adding another piece to a giant puzzle!

Henrietta Leavitt was a scientist. She worked at Harvard in the early 1900s. She found a way to measure the distance of certain stars by how their brightness changed over time. Her work helped astronomers learn about the Milky Way. One of them was Harlow Shapley. He measured distances to groups of stars across the Milky Way. Some of these groups formed a sphere around one place in space. This sphere seemed to be the center of the Milky Way. This showed that the sun was not in the center of the galaxy.

Henrietta Leavitt

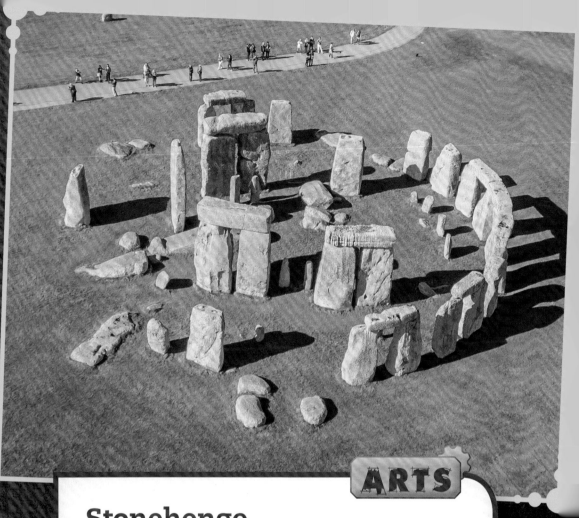

Stonehenge

People may have studied the moon and stars since the Stone Age. Many ancient structures from all over the world seem to relate to the paths of the sun and moon in the sky. One of the most famous is Stonehenge in England. At first, people thought that the monument was only a work of art. Then, they noticed that the stones line up with the sun and moon at different times of the year.

People used to think that all the stars that could be seen in the sky were part of the Milky Way. A scientist named Edwin Hubble changed that.

Hubble studied a small **nebula** (NEB-yoo-luh) named Andromeda (an-DRAW-muh-duh). He found that it wasn't just gas and dust. It was a group of stars that were much farther away than anything else in the Milky Way. It was a whole galaxy of its own. Scientists had to revise what they thought they knew about space.

Hubble changed the way scientists look at the Milky Way. We now know that there are more than 100 billion galaxies. Some are smaller than the Milky Way. Others are much larger. The Milky Way is just a small part of the **universe**.

nebula

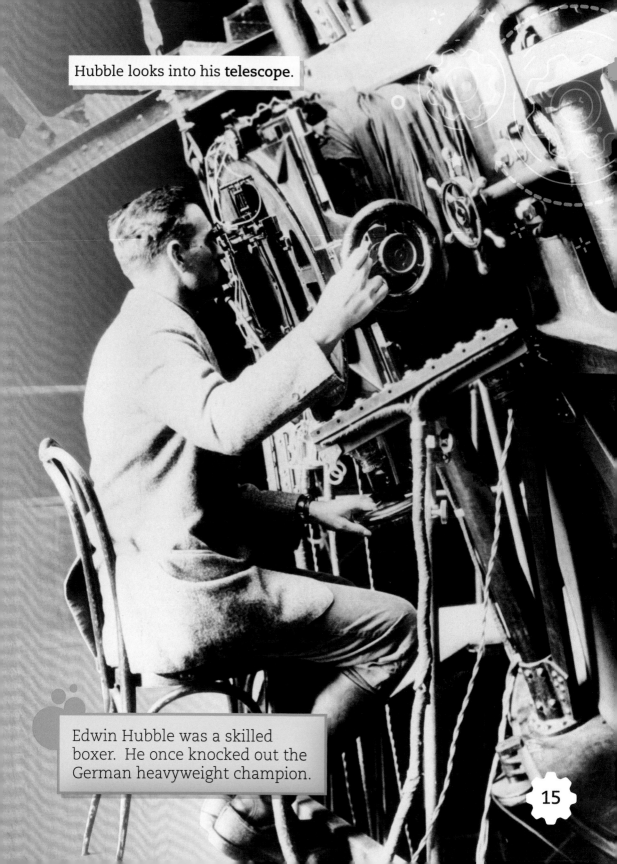

Hubble looks into his **telescope**.

Edwin Hubble was a skilled boxer. He once knocked out the German heavyweight champion.

A Scientist's Toolkit

Scientists use many kinds of tools to study the Milky Way. One very useful tool is the telescope. **Optical** telescopes are used to study light and look at things that are very far away.

The first **telescope** was invented in the 1600s. Its images were small and fuzzy. Galileo Galilei took this design and made it much stronger. With his device, people were able to see craters on the moon! Over time, more powerful telescopes were built. Glass lenses and mirrors were added. The view of space became clearer.

Astronomers learn a lot from studying starlight from a telescope. They can find out what a star is made of. They can find out how big it is. They can tell how fast a star is traveling. They can also find out where it is going. There is a lot to learn from just a little bit of light!

June to August is the best time to view the Milky Way.

Two of Galileo's first telescopes are kept in a museum.

Galileo Galilei

17

Scientists use **radio waves** to study sound in space. A radio telescope is made of two parts—an antenna and a receiver. The antenna points up at the sky. It collects radio waves as they come down to Earth. Then, the receiver turns the waves into data that can be studied. These tools can even create pictures from the noises they detect.

Radio waves from space can be large. Some can be as long as a football field! For scientists to capture these signals, they need antennas that are large. The tools look like huge bowls.

To make even larger telescopes, they group smaller ones together. The telescopes act like one giant antenna. This is called an *array*. There are many arrays set up all over the world.

radio telescope array in New Mexico

The Very Long Baseline Array (VLBA)

Brewster, Wash.

Pie Town and
Los Alamos, N.M.

Owens Valley, Calif.

Kitt Peak, Ariz.

Fort Davis, Texas

North Liberty, Iowa

Hancock, N.H.

Mauna Kea, Hawaii

St. Croix, V.I.

1,000 km

1,000 miles

ENGINEERING

Hooray for Arrays

The Very Long Baseline Array (VLBA) was
made in 1993. Ten radio antennas were set up
around the United States. They combined to
make one array. Each one collects data from
the sky above it. Today, it is being used to map
the Milky Way.

X-ray and **gamma-ray** telescopes study the hottest objects in space—usually the sun and some stars. These tools are placed on very tall mountains.

Infrared telescopes are used to look at things that give off heat. These tools help people see into the centers of galaxies. They also look into clouds of gas and dust in space, where stars are born. To work best, they must be kept cold. So they are usually placed in space.

The Hubble Telescope is an example of a reflecting telescope. It uses mirrors to make images. It is the biggest space telescope. It is part of the Hubble spacecraft. The Hubble spacecraft is about the size of a school bus! It has been **orbiting** Earth at about 8 kilometers (5 miles) per second since 1990.

The Hubble takes pictures of space. It faces away from Earth. This lets it see deep into the universe. It has taken pictures of planets, stars, comets, and more. Scientists have learned a lot about the Milky Way from this tool.

The Hubble spacecraft orbits Earth.

This X-ray telescope is tested to survive in extremely cold temperatures.

TECHNOLOGY

Cool Tool

Everything on Earth gives off heat. Even things that are very cold, such as ice, give off some heat. That is why it can be hard to use infrared telescopes on Earth. They pick up the heat of their surroundings.

Scientists have another tool that they use to chart the Milky Way. It is an optical telescope called Gaia (GY-uh). It was sent into space in 2013. Its mission is to help make a better map of the Milky Way. It will map more than one billion stars.

Gaia gathers data about the things that it sees. It maps where stars are in space. It also maps how fast they are moving. It records the brightness and temperature of each star. It also finds out what each star is made of. This data is sent back to Earth. Scientists use the data to create a three-dimensional map of the Milky Way.

So far, Gaia has found 400 million stars that we did not know about! The Milky Way is bigger than we thought.

Gaia will have more than one million gigabytes worth of information about the Milky Way by the end of its tour in space. It would take 200,000 DVDs to store that much information!

Each dot on this map
shows an asteroid
that Gaia has found.

The Next Frontier

So, what is left to learn about the Milky Way? A lot! Yes, we do know many things about our galaxy. But we have only seen and mapped 1 percent of it. We have just begun to find out all the secrets that wait for us.

New discoveries are made every day. Recently, a group of scientists found new evidence of a huge black hole at the center of the Milky Way. This hole is four million times the mass of our sun.

A cluster of stars seems to orbit this black hole just as Earth orbits the sun. It takes 16 Earth years for these stars to orbit. This is the best evidence scientists have that the black hole exists.

This drawing shows the Milky Way (top) and two other galaxies surrounded by gas.

The bright spots in this infrared image are a group of stars in the middle of the Milky Way.

The Milky Way's dark matter halo is about 90 percent of our galaxy's mass.

Mapping the Milky Way is a project that will never end. It is like a puzzle with an unknown number of pieces. Each new discovery might take many years. But each time we find something new, it is exciting! It is a chance to gain a better picture of this place in space that we call home. Who knows what we will learn in the years to come?

When it comes to mapping the Milky Way, scientists know one thing for sure. They know that there is still a lot they do not know! But as time goes on, technology will improve. Tools that we use to map the Milky Way will also get better. This will help us study space in ways that we cannot even imagine.

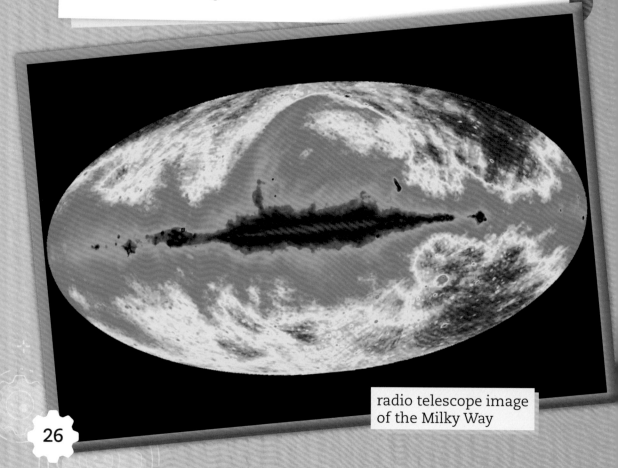

radio telescope image of the Milky Way

Astronomers stand in the dish of a radio telescope.

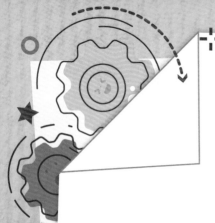

STEAM CHALLENGE

Define the Problem

Scientists have developed a new infrared telescope. The images will provide more data about stars and the Milky Way. Now, they must use a spacecraft to send it into space. Your task is to design and build a shield for the spacecraft. It must block radiation from the sun and other objects in space.

 Constraints: You may only use types of paper to build the shield.

 Criteria: You will test your design by placing the shield on top of a flashlight. The materials must prevent the light from traveling through.

Research and Brainstorm

How do infrared telescopes work? Why are infrared telescopes used mostly in space? What types of materials absorb light?

Design and Build

Sketch your design. What purpose will each part serve? Which types of paper will work best? Build the model.

Test and Improve

Test your design by shining a light on the model. Did the materials work to shield the light? How can you improve it? Modify your design, and try again.

Reflect and Share

Could it work with less paper? Does the model also shield heat? How could you test this? How do you think scientists test space instruments on Earth?

Glossary

astronomer—a person who studies the stars, planets, and other things in space

atmosphere—the mass of air that surrounds Earth

chart—to make a map of something

galaxy—one of the large groups of stars that make up the universe

gamma-ray—a type of invisible ray given off by radioactive things

halo—a circle of light around an object

infrared—using light that cannot be seen by human eyes

nebula—a cloud of gas or dust in space that can sometimes be seen at night

optical—relating to or using light

orbiting—following a curved path around something else

radio waves— electromagnetic radiation with wavelengths longer than infrared light

solar system—the sun and the planets that move around it

telescope—a device that uses lenses to make distant objects appear closer and larger

universe—all of space and everything in it

Index

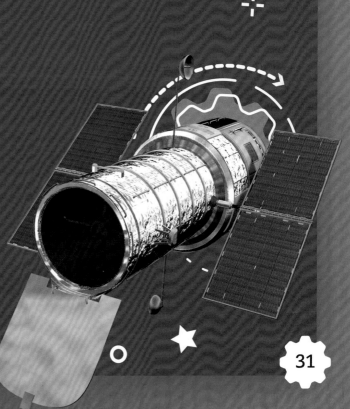

Do you want to explore space?
Here are some tips to get you started.

"A lot of the Milky Way is still a mystery. That's what makes studying it so challenging and exciting! If this is something you want to do, you need a strong background in math, physics, and chemistry. These are difficult subjects, so get ready to study hard!" —**Mark Reid, Senior Radio Astronomer**

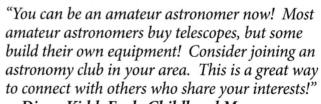

"You can be an amateur astronomer now! Most amateur astronomers buy telescopes, but some build their own equipment! Consider joining an astronomy club in your area. This is a great way to connect with others who share your interests!" —**Diane Kidd, Early Childhood Manager, National Air and Space Museum**